Authentic DIXIELAND

Original Arrangements for Dixieland Band

Selection No.	CONTENTS	Page No.
2	BASIN STREET BLUES	4
11	COPENHAGEN	22
5	THE DARKTOWN STRUTTERS' BALL	10
3	FIDGETY FEET	6
1	HIGH SOCIETY	2
6	MUSKRAT RAMBLE	12
8	NATIONAL EMBLEM	16
4	PANAMA	8
7	SENSATION	14
10	SOUTH RAMPART STREET PARADE	19
9	WABASH BLUES	18

INSTRUMENTATION	
PIANO	TROMBONE
CLARINET	STRING BASS
TRUMPET	DRUMS
TENOR SAX	GUITAR (Banjo)

❶HIGH SOCIETY

By PORTER STEELE, WALTER MELROSE
Arr. by Bill Howard

Trombone

3

② BASIN STREET BLUES

Trombone

By SPENCER WILLIAMS
Arr. by Bill Howard

❸ FIDGETY FEET

By D.J. LA ROCCA, LARRY SHIELDS
Arr. by Leroy Holmes

Trombone

2364

4 PANAMA

By WILLIAM H. TYERS
Arr. Leroy Holmes

Trombone

2364

❺ THE DARKTOWN STRUTTERS' BALL

Trombone

By SHELTON BROOKS
Arr. by Leroy Holmes

⑥ MUSKRAT RAMBLE

Trombone

(>) DENOTES LONG NOTE
(∧) DENOTES SHORT NOTE

By RAY GILBERT, EDWARD "KID" ORY
Arr. by Deane Kincaide

2364

⑦ SENSATION

By E.B. EDWARDS
Arr. by Leroy Holmes

Trombone

⑧ NATIONAL EMBLEM

Trombone

By E.E. BAGLEY
Arr. by Deane Kincaide

❾ WABASH BLUES

Trombone

By DAVE RINGLE, FRED MEINKEN
Arr. by Leroy Holmes

⑩ SOUTH RAMPART STREET PARADE

19

By RAY BAUDUC, BOB HAGGART
Arr. by Deane Kincaide

Trombone

2364

20

2364

⑪ COPENHAGEN

By WALTER MELROSE, CHARLIE DAVIS
Arr. by Bill Howard

Trombone